Surprise in the Middle

Surprise in the Middle

Listening Activities Take an Unexpected Turn

ISBN 0-936110-24-4
Library of Congress Control Number: 2001 130567

Tin Man Press
Phone: 800-676-0459
Fax: 888-515-1764

www.tinmanpress.com

Contents

Introduction

The element of surprise can be a wonderful thing. In this book, it is the motivational tool, the hook, the carrot, for getting children to listen carefully. As children do more and more of these activities, they'll become better and better listeners.

Each activity begins with a set of oral directions telling students to make certain marks on their paper.

Then, midway into the activity, you get to say "Surprise! You have just started a drawing of ..." and those seemingly meaningless marks have led children into a drawing they hadn't dreamed of making. In other words, each activity heads one way, stops, makes a turn, and finishes in a very different way.

When you think of it, this isn't easy. In every case, students begin their work with a blank piece of paper. Then they must wait for you to tell them what to draw and where to put it on the paper. Careful listening is the only way to successfully complete each challenge.

After the disciplined listening, and after the announcement of the "surprise in the middle," each activity proceeds to a looser, more creative stage. That's when children get to depart from the structure that has been presented and use their own ideas and decisions to finish the drawings.

In order to give directions for placing lines here and there, it has been necessary to establish certain measurement criteria. Rather than formal measurements—inches and centimeters—we have chosen to stick to the tried and true: the hand. Therefore, you will find phrases such as "two finger widths" and "as tall as your pointer finger" in practically every activity.

If you are working with older students, feel free to substitute a half-inch for "one finger's width." Also—and this is important—the measurements, whether in half inches or finger widths, do not have to be exact.

You will also find phrases such as "up and down" and "straight across." With older students, you could (and should) substitute "vertical" and "horizontal."

The book begins with a couple of easy activities to get children comfortable with the concept before going on to more difficult challenges. You may need to repeat some of the directions, and that's fine. When students make erroneous marks—and they will, from time to time—it's okay for them to use their erasers. For that reason, pencils should be used for all activities.

Most of these activities should take about fifteen or twenty minutes to do. (Students may want to spend more time embellishing their drawings later.)

One final note: We have given each activity a title, but that's really just for your benefit. Students should never be told the name of the activity in advance. Remember, each activity is a surprise!

— Greta and Ted Rasmussen

Go Fly a Kite

Say to students:

Position your paper so that one of the short sides is nearest to you, and listen carefully to my instructions before you do anything.

The set-up drawing

Your first job will be to lay the pointer finger of the hand you DON'T write with flat on your paper, sticking up from the bottom edge, about in the middle. Most of that finger should be touching the paper. Then, draw around that finger. Do this now.

Now, you'll be drawing a circle that is a little bit wider than the finger shape. It should touch the very top of your finger outline. Draw the circle now.

Near the top of your paper, toward the right, you'll be drawing a diamond shape that is about as long as the finger shape you just drew. The bottom part of the diamond should be pointing down toward your finger shape. Draw that now.

Next, starting at the bottom part of the diamond, draw a little wiggly line that is about as long as the diamond shape. It should point in the direction of the finger outline.

SURPRISE! You've just started a drawing of a little person flying a big kite. But there are some problems.

The first problem is that the little person (which is the finger-and-circle shape) needs an arm and a hand holding a string that goes up to the middle of the kite. Draw the arm, hand, and string.

Now that we know the kite is not going to get away, I can tell you that the kite is decorated with a big, scary face that fills up almost all of the diamond shape. Draw the scary face now.

Now, finish your finger-person any way you like, but try to make it look like the person is watching the kite.

And what kind of a day is it? Is the sun shining? Are there clouds in the sky? Add as many details as you can. Good luck.

A finished version

The Robot

Say to students:

Position your paper so that one of the long sides is nearest to you, and wait for my instructions before you begin.

First, bring the bottom edge of your paper to the top edge and make a fold. Then, smooth the paper out.

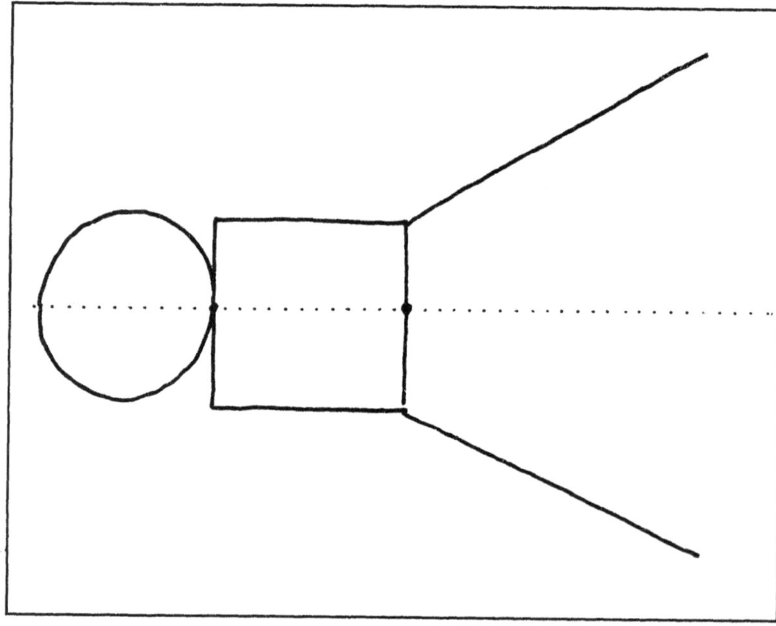

The set-up drawing

Now, I'll want you to put a tiny dot in the middle of the fold line. Make the dot now.

Next, half way between the dot you just made and the left edge of your paper, on the fold line, you'll be making another small dot. Make the dot now.

Now, you'll be making a square that fits between the two dots. In other words, the dots will touch two sides of the square. Half the square should be above the fold line and half should be below it. Make the square now.

Next, starting at the top right corner of the square, I'll want you to draw a line that goes toward the top right corner of the paper. It should stop about three finger widths from the corner. Draw the line now.

Now, starting at the bottom right corner of the square, you'll be drawing a line that goes toward the bottom right corner of the paper. It should also stop about three finger widths from the corner. Draw the line now.

Next, you'll be making a circle. It should touch the left dot and almost touch the left edge of your paper. Half of the circle should be above the fold line and half below the fold line. Make the circle now.

Finally, turn your paper so that the circle is at the top.

SURPRISE! You've just started a drawing of a robot. The circle is the robot's head, the square is its body, and the lines are part of its legs, which as you can see, are spaced out so that the robot has really good balance.

Let's add some details.

First, the robot needs stronger legs. Use the lines that are there as edges of the legs. Finish the legs now.

The robot has skinny arms that are made up of several pieces so they'll bend in many directions. Draw the arms now and put them in interesting positions.

Oh, and there's a little TV screen on the robot's chest. The screen shows what the robot is looking at. That could be a scene of anything you'd like. Show that now.

Now, let's think about the robot's face. How do you want to draw it? I'll leave that up to you, and when you finish, put in lots of other details. What about feet? What about hands? What about bolts and wires? What about an antenna? You decide. Good luck!

A finished version

Design I

Say to students:

First, place your paper so that one of the long sides is nearest to you, and listen carefully to my instructions before you draw.

Your first job will be to draw four straight lines of different lengths. Scatter them around on the paper any way you like but don't let them touch each other. Remember, the lines can point in any direction. Draw the four straight lines now.

Next, I'll want you to connect the end of one line with the end of another line by making a wiggly line. Do this now.

Then, I'll want you to draw another wiggly line that starts at the same place as the first wiggly line. It should connect with the end of one of the other straight lines. Draw the second wiggly line now.

Next, find a place where nothing has been drawn and invent an interesting shape made entirely of curves. Draw that shape now.

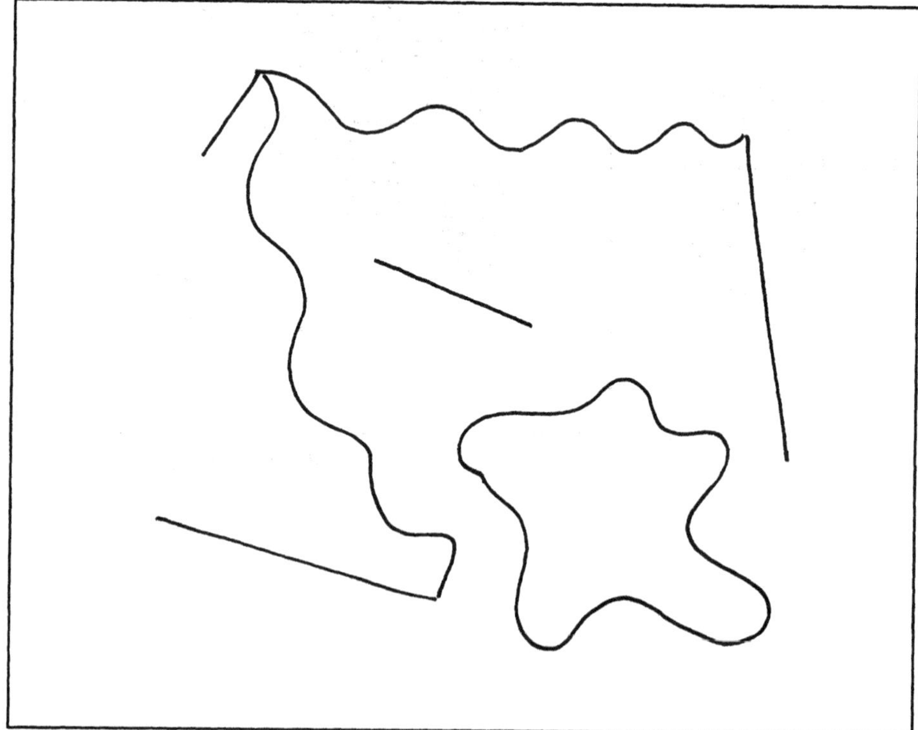

The set-up drawing

SURPRISE! You've just started an interesting design!

Look at the design you've made so far. Turn the paper around and view it from all four sides. Which side do you like best? Put your initials in the lower right corner so that we'll know how to view it.

Now, find a place in your design where you could put one dark circle that would make the design look more balanced. The size of the circle is up to you, but you should darken it in with your pencil. Draw the circle now.

Then, starting from the middle of the curved shape you made, draw a long curved line that goes around the dark circle and attaches to the end of one of the straight lines.

Finally, finish your design in any way you like. How about adding more shapes? How about including some dots or stripes? How about some shaded areas? You decide, but be sure your design looks lively.

A finished version

On the Train

Say to students:

Position your paper so that one of the long sides is nearest to you, and listen to my instructions before you do anything.

First, bring the bottom edge of your paper to the top edge and make a fold. Press down on the fold and leave the paper folded. Next, bring the edge with the fold up to the top edge and fold again. Press down on the fold. Then, open the paper up and smooth it out. Your paper should now be divided into four sections that go all the way from the left to the right.

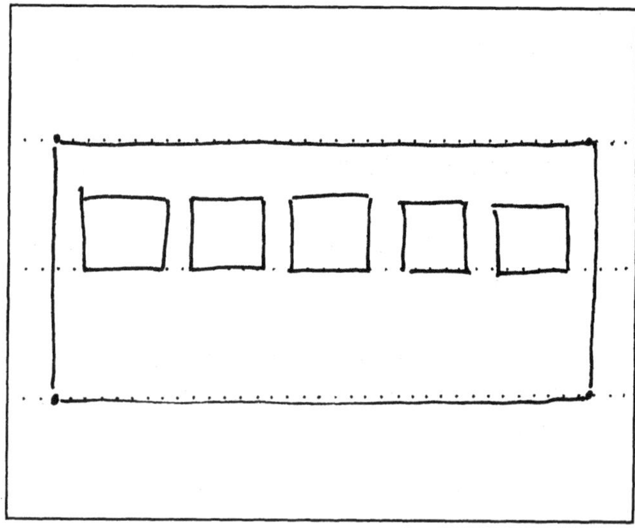

The set-up drawing

Your first job will be to make a tiny dot on the top fold line. You should put it about two finger widths in from the left side of your paper. Make the dot now.

Now, you'll be making a tiny dot on the top fold line again. But you should put this dot two finger widths in from the right side of your paper. Make the dot now.

Next, you'll be making another small dot on the bottom fold line. You should put it two finger widths in from the left side of your paper. Make the dot now.

Then, you'll be making one more tiny dot on the bottom fold line again. You should put this one two finger widths in from the right side of your paper. Make the dot now.

Now connect the dots with straight lines to make a big rectangle.

Next, inside the big rectangle, you'll be drawing five squares that are all about the same size. The squares should have their bottom edges on the middle fold line. There should be a little space between each square, and when you are finished, they should be spaced out evenly from near the left edge of the big rectangle to near the right edge. In other words, you'll be making a row of squares. The squares don't have to be drawn perfectly. Draw the five squares on the middle fold line now.

SURPRISE! You've just started a drawing of a train car!

The squares are windows, and this train car is full. There's something different going on in each window. Now, it's your job to finish each scene.

In the far left window, a small boy is looking out at the scenery. He has big eyes and curly hair. Draw him now.

In the next window, a girl has opened a table in front of her and is eating lunch. You can see the girl, the tabletop, and her lunch. Show this.

In the third window, a man is sleeping. His face is toward the window, and he has a very bushy beard. Show him sleeping.

In the fourth window, a woman wearing a tiny hat is reading a newspaper. Draw her now.

It'll be up to you to decide what to draw in the remaining window, but remember, this train car is packed. Go ahead and put someone in the window.

Your last job will be to make the train look more real. How about wheels? How about showing parts of the train cars in front and behind? Is the name of the railroad on the side of the car? And don't forget to put this train on a track! Good luck.

A finished version

The Rug

Say to students:

Place one of the short sides of the paper nearest to you, and get ready for lots of folding. In this activity, it is very important to press down hard on the folds to make good creases. Okay, here we go.

First, bring the bottom edge of your paper to the top edge. Fold it and crease it. Then, with the paper still folded, bring the left side to the right side and press down on that fold. With the paper still folded, bring the bottom edge to the top edge. Fold it and crease it. Finally, bring the left side to the right side and press down on that fold.

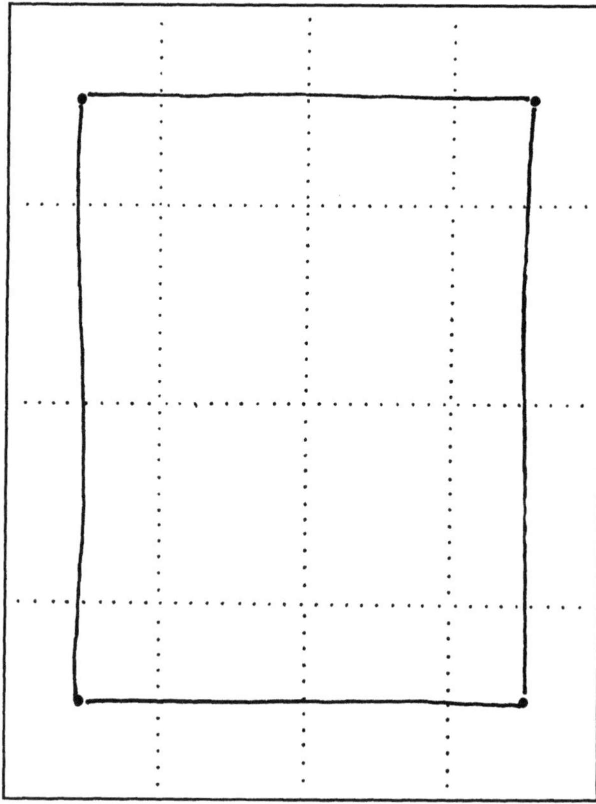

The set-up drawing

Now, open up your paper and smooth it out. You should have sixteen sections that have been made by the folds. Be sure that one of the short sides of the paper is still nearest to you.

Your first mark will be a dot that I want you to make in the middle of the top left section. Make the dot now.

Now, make a dot in the middle of the top right section.

Then, make a dot in the middle of the lower left section.

Then, make a dot in the middle of the lower right section.

Next, connect the top left dot with the top right dot by drawing a straight line.

Then, connect the top right dot with the bottom right dot by drawing a straight line.

Then, connect the bottom left dot with the bottom right dot by drawing a straight line.

Finally, connect the top left dot with the bottom left dot by drawing a straight line.

SURPRISE! You've just started a drawing of a very pretty rug!

The outline is there, but the design is missing! To start making your rug design, you'll need to draw little circles about the size of a pea at the places where the fold lines meet. You should have nine little circles when you finish. Do this now.

Next, draw a small diamond shape around every circle.

What else can you do to make the rug look more like a rug? Well, some rugs have fringe at the top and bottom ends. Give your rug some fringe.

Finally, think about some other ways you can improve your rug design. You might think about drawing some straight lines between the diamonds. Or you could add some big circles in the middle of some sections. You might want to darken some areas, or you could make certain lines thicker. You could even draw some animals, or flowers.

Decisions, decisions. You decide.

A finished version

Spooky Halloween

Say to students:

First, place your paper so that one of the long sides is nearest to you, and listen to my directions before you start to draw.

Your first job will be to draw a table. I'll want you to draw the legs of the table first. You'll be making just two legs, not four, since you'll be looking at the table from the side. The legs should start at the bottom edge of your paper—sort of in the middle. You should space them apart about the length of your pointer finger, and make them almost that tall, too. Draw the two legs now.

The set-up drawing

Next, you'll be making the top of the table. The tabletop should touch the legs, of course, and ought to be straight across. Do this now.

Then, on top of the table, you'll be drawing a big circle. The circle should be about half as wide as the table. Draw the circle now.

Now, over toward the left side of the paper, about half way up, you'll be drawing two little circles. Each one of them should be about the size of a pea. Put them close together, but not touching. They should be side-by-side—not on top of each other. Draw the circles now.

Next, I'll want you to draw a wiggly line that comes down from the top of the paper, somewhere on the right side. Make it about as long as one of the table legs.

Now, anywhere in the top half of your paper, draw three capital letter V's a little larger than the two side-by-side circles. You can scatter them around, but they shouldn't touch each other or any other shape.

SURPRISE! You've just started a drawing of a very spooky room in a Halloween haunted house!

The circle is a jack-o'-lantern. Give it a scary face.

There is a big, hairy spider hanging from the wiggly line. Draw it.

The two little circles belong to a ghost. They are the eyes. Finish the ghost by giving it an outline of some kind.

And the V's? They are bats. Do something to the V's to make them look like bats.

Finally, add as many other details as you can to make the room look even more scary. Are there cobwebs? Are there scary shadows on the wall? You decide. Good luck!

A finished version

The Messy Room

Say to students:

Position your paper so that one of the long sides is nearest to you, and listen to my instructions before you do anything.

First, bring the bottom edge of your paper to the top edge and make a fold. Then, smooth the paper out.

Next, you'll be drawing a skinny rectangle. The bottom of the rectangle should be on the fold line. The rectangle should be about the size of a stick of gum, with the long sides straight across, not up and down. It should be in the middle of your paper. Remember, it goes on the fold line. Draw the rectangle now.

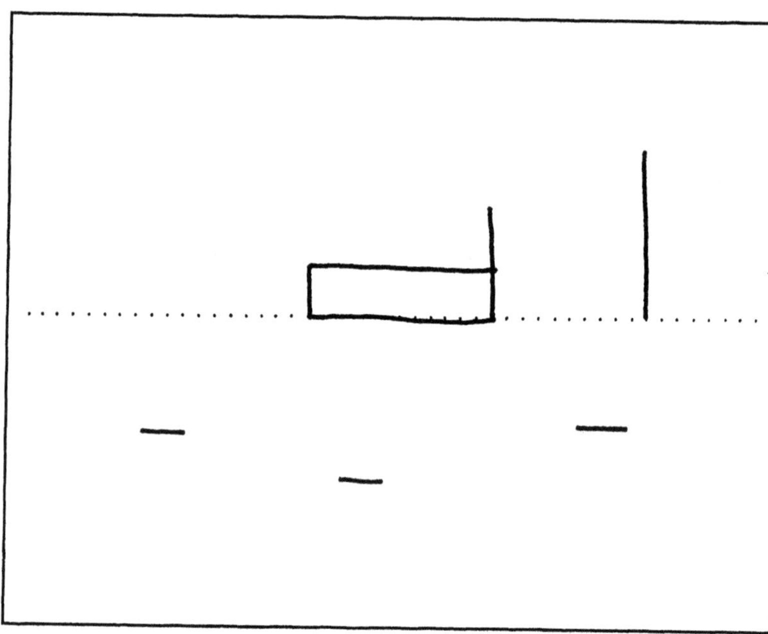

The set-up drawing

Now, starting at the upper right corner of the rectangle, I'll be asking you to make a line that goes straight up from that corner. It should be about as long as one of the short sides of the rectangle. Draw this line now.

Next, about half way between the right edge of the rectangle and the right edge of the paper, I'll want you to draw a straight up-and-down line. The line should be about as tall as your pointer finger. It should start on the fold line and go up. Draw the line now.

Finally, I'm going to ask you to make three short straight-across lines. Each of them should be about one finger width wide. You should put them in the lower half of the paper, not too close to each other or to the edges. Make the three short lines now.

SURPRISE! You've just started a drawing of a very, very messy bedroom.

The rectangle is the bed, as seen from the side. Since I said this was a messy room, of course the bed hasn't been made. How would this look? Is there a wad of covers at the foot of the bed? Is a sheet hanging down over the side? Are there pillows on the bed? You decide how to draw the bed so that it looks messy.

The straight up-and-down line on your paper is the beginning of a floor lamp. Someone has brushed against it so the shade is slightly crooked. Finish drawing the lamp.

One of the short lines is really one edge of a book that someone has dropped on the floor. Draw it, and if you can, make it look like the book is open.

Another of the short lines is the sole of a shoe. The other shoe must be under the bed. Finish drawing the shoe, and by the way, it has laces.

A baseball cap has been thrown on the floor, too. Use the remaining line as part of the cap.

Finally, show the bed and the lamp sitting on a big oval rug. Then add more details. Is there a window in the room? Are there pictures on the wall? Since this is a messy room, I'll bet the pictures might be a little crooked. How about some other stuff on the floor? You decide.

A finished version

Danger

Say to students:

Position your paper so that one of the long sides is nearest to you, and listen carefully to each instruction before you start to draw.

The set-up drawing

The first thing you're going to do is to draw a line all the way across the paper. The line should be about four finger widths up from the bottom edge. Make the line now.

Next, think of an orange sliced in half with the sliced part on the line. How would that look? I want you to try drawing it. It should go on the left part of the line, near the edge of the paper, and it should be about as big as a real orange half. Draw it now.

Now, you're going to draw something else on the line—a little rectangle, about the size of a postage stamp. Make it so that one of the long sides is on the line, and put it close to, but not touching, the right edge of the paper. Remember, it has to go on the line. Do this now.

Now, still on the line but a little to the left of the rectangle, you'll be drawing an oval about as big as a raisin. One of the long sides of the oval should be on the line. Draw it now.

Your next job involves attaching a circle to the big half-orange shape you made. This circle should be about three finger widths across. It should connect to the right side of the half-orange shape, a little bit up from the line. Draw the circle now.

Finally, make five or six small circles in the rectangle on the right. Be sure to scatter them around.

SURPRISE! You've just started a drawing of a cat ready to pounce on a mouse ready to eat some delicious-looking cheese.

Of course, the big shape on the left is the cat. The half-circle is its body, and the circle is its head. But it's missing a face, ears, tail, paws—even whiskers! Draw these things now.

The middle shape is the body of a mouse. Finish the mouse now, and don't forget that the mouse is looking at the cheese, not at the cat.

And that rectangle on the right is the cheese. Try making it look thicker by showing part of the top and one of the sides. It's a big chunk of cheese, isn't it?

I forgot to tell you that this little drama is taking place in a kitchen. It'll be your job to finish the picture so that we know it's a kitchen. Is all of the action taking place in front of a stove or a refrigerator or under a table? You decide. Of course, the area below the straight-across line is the floor.

Also, if there is time, go back and work on the cat. Does it have stripes or spots? Does it have long hair or short hair?

This picture is waiting for you to put in all the details! Good luck.

A finished version

Out of this World

Say to students:

Position your paper so that one of the long sides is nearest to you, and listen to my instructions before you draw.

First, a little more than half way up on your paper, you'll be making a wavy line that goes all the way across the paper, from the left edge to the right edge. Draw the line now.

Next, below the line but touching it, I'll want you to draw a big letter V. The V should be about as tall as your little finger is long. You can put it anywhere below the line. Draw the big letter V now.

Now, you'll be drawing two smaller V's, below the line but still touching it. They also can go anywhere you wish, but they must still touch the line. Draw the two smaller V's now.

Your next job will be to draw a large oval, about the size of your hand. It should go somewhere below the wavy line, but shouldn't touch the V's or the edges of your paper. The oval should look like it goes across, not up and down. Draw the large oval now.

Now, above the wavy line, I'll want you to draw three circles. Each of them should be about as big as a penny. Put them about half way between the wavy line and the top edge of the paper, and space them out. Draw the three little circles now.

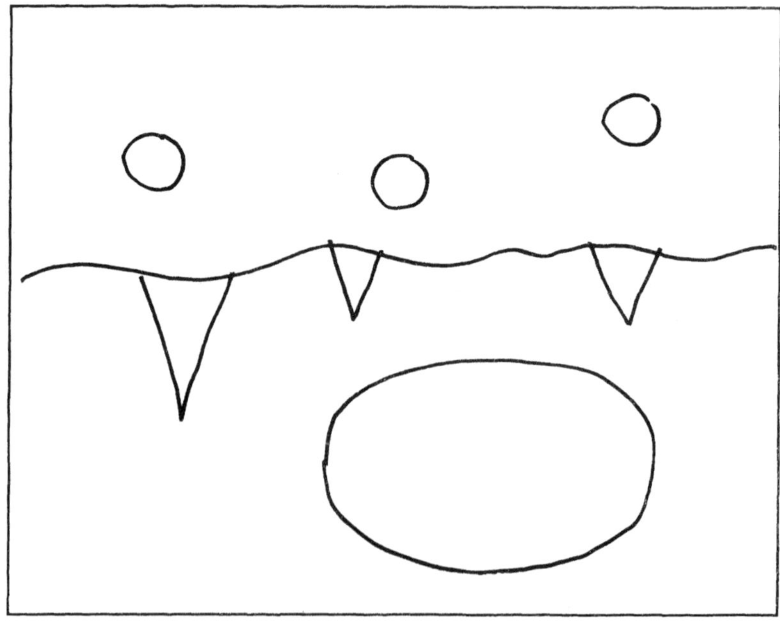

The set-up drawing

SURPRISE! Turn your paper upside down and you'll find you've just started a drawing of a spaceship arriving to explore a weird planet in another galaxy.

What are the V's that are now upside down? They are volcanoes! One is making a lot of smoke, one is making a little smoke, and one none at all. Draw the smoke.

Your spaceship, which is the oval, has a big antenna and several round windows. Show this now.

One of the circles below the wavy line is the head of a strange animal that lives on this planet. Finish it.

Another of the circles is just a hole, with a scary snake-like creature poking its head out of it. Draw that, too.

The third circle is the head of one of the strange people who inhabit this planet. Take some time to draw him or her or it now.

A finished version

Uh-oh. Another spaceship has just come into the picture. It's so much larger than your spaceship that most of it is outside of the picture. Draw what it would look like, and be sure to include a big window in the cockpit so we can see who is flying it.

Now, it's time to add some other details. How about drawing some people looking out of your spaceship? How about adding some stars? It's up to you to make this picture truly out of this world. Good luck.

Sue's Twos

Say to students:

Position your paper so that one of the long sides is nearest to you, and listen carefully to my instructions before you do anything.

First, bring the bottom edge of your paper to the top edge and make a fold. Then, smooth the paper out.

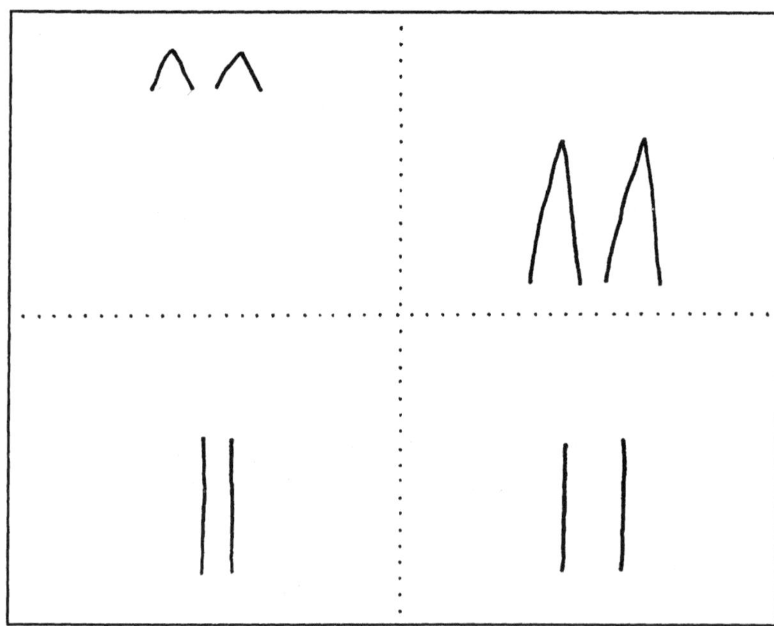

The set-up drawing

Next, fold the paper in half once more, left to right. Then, smooth the paper out. Be sure that one of the long sides is nearest to you. Your paper is now divided into four rectangles, isn't it?

In the upper left rectangle, I'll want you to draw two upside-down letter V's next to each other. They should be about one finger width tall, and should be about a finger width apart. You should put them in the middle of the rectangle, near the top. Make the two upside-down V's now.

In the upper right rectangle, you'll be drawing two more upside down V's, but these should be much taller—about as tall as your little finger. They should go in the middle of the rectangle, near the bottom, and they should be close together but not touching. Make the bigger upside-down V's now.

In the lower left rectangle, I'll want you to draw two up-and-down lines that look like the number eleven. The lines should be as tall as your little finger, and about one finger width apart. They should be placed a little bit below the middle of the rectangle. Make the two lines now.

In the lower right rectangle, you'll be drawing another pair of up-and-down lines. These should be about as tall as the other ones but spaced twice as far apart. Place them in about the same position as the first pair, a little bit below the middle of the rectangle. Make the two lines now.

SURPRISE! You've just started drawing a page from a photo album belonging to a girl named Sue.

Sue is going to tell you what's in each picture. It'll be your job to use the marks you have just made as part of your picture. But there is one rule: Your drawings should not touch the fold lines or the edges of the paper.

Here is her description of the upper left photograph. "My cat Oscar has big eyes and three funny spots on his face."

This is what she had to say about the upper right photograph. "On our vacation last year, we saw two birds with long legs and pointy beaks."

Here is her description of the lower left photograph. "The tree outside my window has very rough bark and a hole in its trunk."

And this is her description of the lower right photograph. "Here is a picture of a sand castle I made last summer at the beach."

Now, draw around each of the pictures to make them look more like photographs in an album. And, if you want to add more details to your pictures, go ahead. Good luck.

A finished version

The Clown

Say to students:

Place your paper so that one of the short sides is nearest to you, and listen carefully to my instructions before you draw.

In the middle of your paper, I'll want you to make a little dot. Make the dot now.

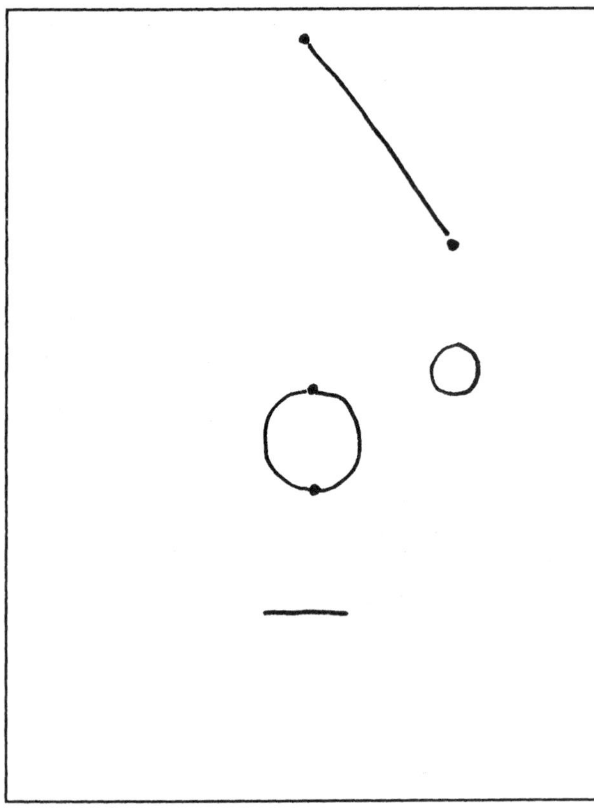

The set-up drawing

Next, you'll be making another dot three finger widths below the first dot. Make the dot now.

Now, you'll be making a circle that fits exactly in between the two dots. Make the circle now.

Next, think of an imaginary line that goes straight across from the top of the circle you just made to the right edge of the paper. Somewhere near the middle of that imaginary line, I'll want you to draw a smaller circle about the size of a penny. The bottom of it should sit on that imaginary line. Draw the smaller circle now.

Next, almost at the top of your paper, in the middle, I'll want you to make another little dot. Make the dot now.

Then, I'll want you to make another dot about three finger widths above the smaller circle. Make the dot now.

Now, connect the two dots you just made with a straight line.

Next, three finger widths below the big circle you drew, you'll be drawing a short line that goes straight across. It should be centered below the circle and be about as wide as the circle. Draw the line now.

SURPRISE! You've just started a drawing of the face of a clown!

The line going up to the top is the side of his hat. Finish the other side of it and draw a line across the bottom so that it looks like it's on his head.

The small circle is his eye, of course, but he needs another eye. Draw that now.

Next, give him a face shape that starts at one of the bottom corners of the hat and loops all the way around to the other side of the hat. Be sure that the short, straight-across line is well inside the face shape.

Of course, the circle is the nose. Darken it in so that it looks even more like a clown's nose.

The short line under the nose is part of his mouth. What you do to the mouth will determine whether he's going to be a sad or a happy clown. Do this now.

Like many clowns, he is having a very bad hair day. His hair sticks out on both sides. Show how that would look.

Finally, there must be other details you'd like to add. Is he wearing a shirt with ruffles? Does he have funny eyebrows? Think of spots, stripes, ears, cheeks, and ... well, you decide.

A finished version

Mystery Animal I

Say to students:

Turn your paper so that one of the long sides is nearest to you, and listen to my instructions before you draw.

You'll begin today by putting a faint little X in the middle of your paper. Do this now.

Now, bring the left edge of the paper over to the X and make a fold. Then, smooth the paper out.

Do the same thing on the right—bring the edge over to the X, make a fold, and smooth the paper out.

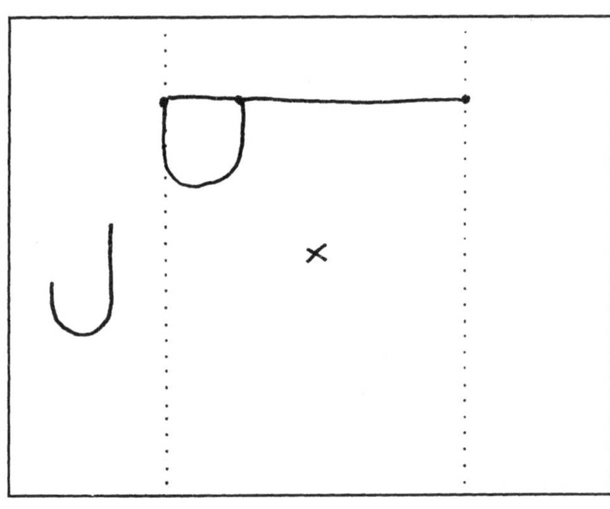

The set-up drawing

Next, look at the fold line on the left side of your paper. You'll be making a tiny dot about three finger widths down from the top edge of your paper. The dot should be on the fold line. Make the dot now.

Now, look at the fold line on the right side of your paper. You'll be making another tiny dot about three finger widths down from the top edge there, too—the same way you did on the left. The dot you make should be on the fold line. Do it now.

Then, draw a line connecting the two dots.

Now, look at the first dot you made—the one on the left—and listen carefully to what I want you to do next.

You'll be making another little dot on the line. It should go three finger widths to the right of the first dot. Make the dot now.

Next, I want you to use both of the dots on the left side as the tops of a big letter U. Make the U now.

Finally, look at the area between the left fold and the left edge of your paper. Half way down in that area, in the middle, you will be making a capital J—but don't give it a top. The J should be about as big as the U you just made.

SURPRISE! You've just started drawing an elephant!

The J is the elephant's trunk and the U is its ear. You can't see both ears because you're looking at the elephant from the side. Do some drawing now to attach the trunk to the elephant's head. Take your time and do a good job.

Next, take a minute to decide just how big to make your elephant, based on what you've already drawn. Use the straight line you drew in the beginning as part of the body. If you want to make the line shorter by erasing, or if you need to make it a little longer, that's okay.

Go ahead and finish the outline of the elephant. Remember, elephants have very thick, sturdy legs.

The elephant needs a tail, too. Elephant tails are quite long, with sort of an oval of hair at the very end. Draw the tail now.

How about an eye? Elephant eyes look almost like our eyes—they even have eyelashes.

Those of you who have seen a real elephant know that their trunks have wrinkles that go straight across. Show that next.

The last thing you'll want to do is to put your elephant into some kind of a setting. For starters, you'd better give it something solid to stand on—since it's so heavy. And since elephants eat green things, put in plants and trees. You might even include an exotic bird or two, clouds in the sky—you decide.

A finished version

Not an Ordinary Ring

Say to students:

Start by placing one of the short sides of the paper nearest to you, and listen carefully before you do anything.

To begin, you'll be putting a faint little X right in the center of your paper. Make the X now.

Next, bring the top edge of the paper down to the little X and make a fold. Then, smooth the paper out.

Then, bring the left edge of your paper over to the little X and make a fold. Then, smooth the paper out.

Now, do the same thing on the right—bring the edge over to the X, make a fold, and smooth the paper out.

Your next job will be to make a little dot at the place where the straight-across fold line meets the left up-and-down fold line. Make the dot now.

Next, you'll be drawing a short line that goes down from that dot. It should point in the direction of the bottom left corner of the paper, and it should be just about as long as your thumbnail. Draw the short line now.

Now, you're going to do the same two steps on the right side of your paper. First, you'll be making a dot at the place where the straight-across fold line meets the up-and-down fold line on the right. Do this now.

Then, draw a short line that goes down from that dot. It should point in the direction of the bottom right corner, and it should be just about as long as your thumbnail. Draw the short line now.

Now, look at the dot on the left. Two finger widths above the dot, on the fold line, I want you to make another little dot.

Now, you'll be doing the same thing on the right. Two finger widths above the dot, on the fold line, you'll be making another dot. Make the dot now.

Next, I want you to put a tiny dot at the top edge of your paper, right in the middle. Do that now.

Finally, think of an imaginary line that goes straight down from the dot you just made and ends up at the fold line below. At that point, I want you to make one more little dot. Do it now.

SURPRISE! You've just started drawing a very fancy diamond ring for the richest lady in the world!

First, draw straight lines to connect every dot with every other dot, even the dots with tails. Some of your lines will cross over other lines, and that's okay.

What you've just drawn is the diamond part of the ring, as seen from the side. And those little short lines coming down the sides of the diamond are the beginnings of the part of the ring that goes around your finger. Draw that big circle now.

To make the ring look even more like a ring, draw a second circle close to the first one so that the ring looks a little thick.

Now, make three more circles near the bottom of your paper.

Congratulations, you've just started three more rings! Turn them into spectacular designs—and make them all different.

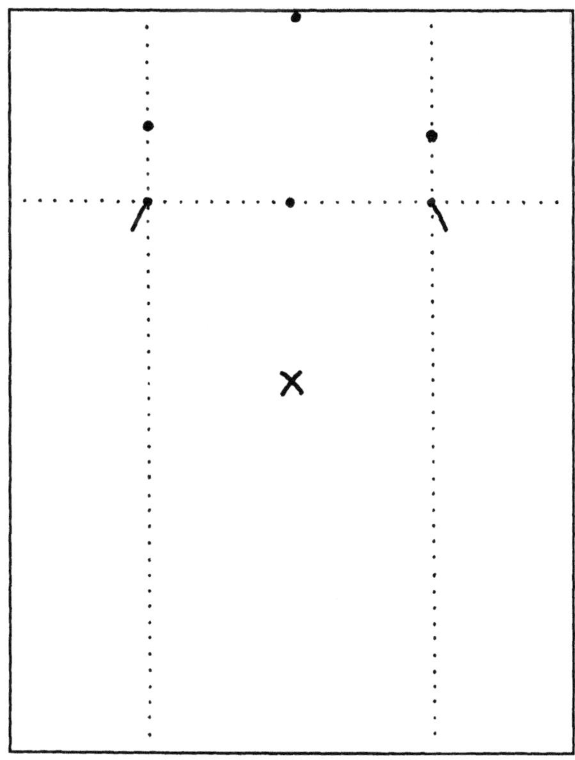

The set-up drawing

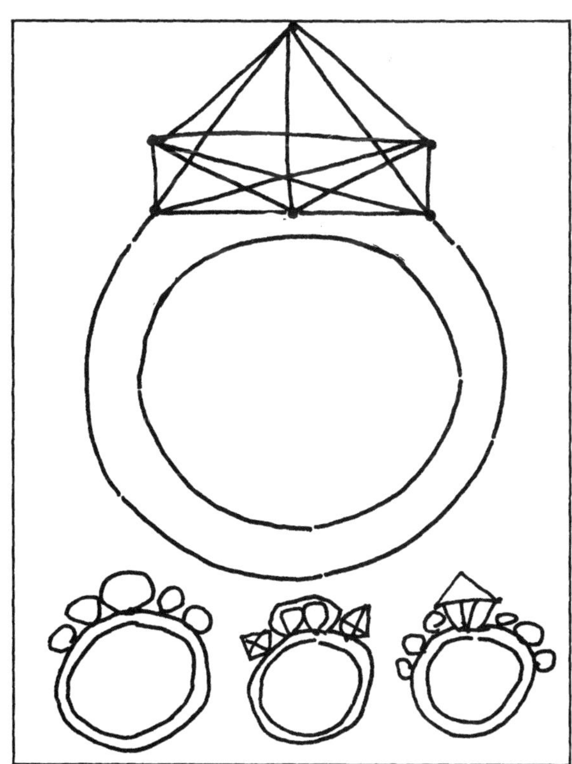

A finished version

The Horse

Say to students:

Position your paper so that one of the long sides is nearest to you, and listen carefully before you do anything.

First, bring the bottom edge of your paper up to the top edge and make a fold. Then open the paper up and smooth it out.

Next, bring the left edge of your paper to the right edge and make another fold. Then open the paper up and smooth it out.

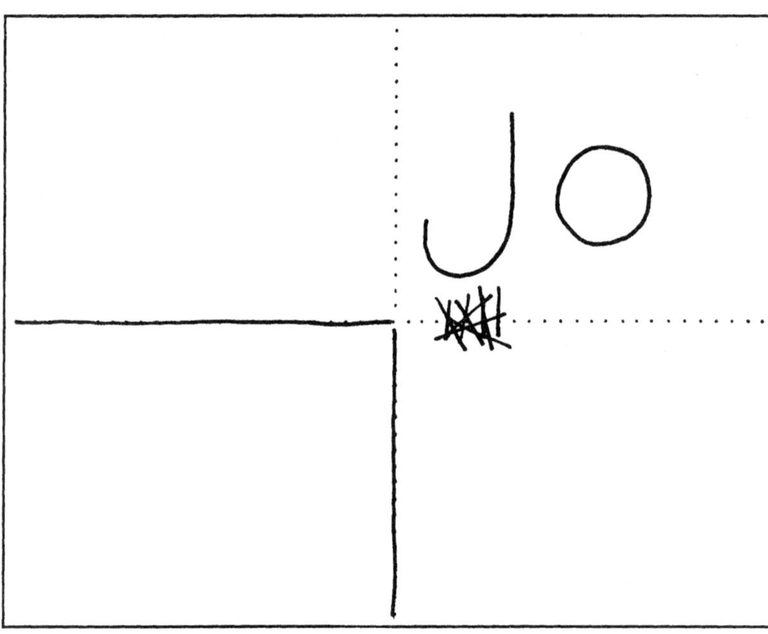

The set-up drawing

Now, look at your paper. You have made four sections, haven't you?

You're going to start your drawing by making a big capital J in the upper right section. The J should be about as tall as your little finger, and it should not have a top line. It should go slightly to the right of the up-and-down fold line, about half way up. Draw it now.

Next, still in the same section, in the very center of the section, you'll be making a capital O. It should be about half as tall as the J. Do this now.

Now, look at the fold lines that form two of the edges of the bottom left section. You'll be drawing lines that follow those two fold lines—the one going across and the one going down. Do this now.

Finally, go back to the top right section again. Under the J, on the fold line, you'll be making a bunch of short lines—at least ten or twelve—that crisscross each other. The lines should be about two finger widths long. Draw them now.

SURPRISE! You've just started a drawing of a person feeding a handful of grass to a horse!

The horse is standing behind a fence. The J is part of the horse's head. The crisscross lines are the grass, and the circle is the person's head. You've already started the fence. Its top is the straight-across line you drew along the fold, and the corner of the fence is the up-and-down line you drew.

First, let me describe the fence. It has an up-and-down post at the corner and three boards that go across. Draw the fence now.

Now, let's think about the horse. The horse is facing the person, which means you're only going to be seeing one of its eyes. Also, it's standing behind the fence, which means you won't be able to see all of its body. Using the letter J as part of its head, draw the horse now. It doesn't have to be perfect. Just give us the idea of a horse.

Finally, let me tell you about the person. You can decide whether it is a boy or a girl or a man or a woman, but the person you draw must be holding the grass, and must be wearing a cowboy hat. The rest is up to you.

It's time for you to think about putting in other details. Can you see the ground? Is the person wearing cowboy boots? Does the horse have a long mane? Get to work right now, and good luck!

A finished version

Design II

Say to students:

First, place your paper so that one of the long sides is nearest to you, and listen carefully to my instructions before you draw.

In the right part of your paper, half way up from the bottom and not too close to the right edge, I'll want you to make a long rectangle about the size and shape of a stick of gum. It can point in any direction. Draw the rectangle now.

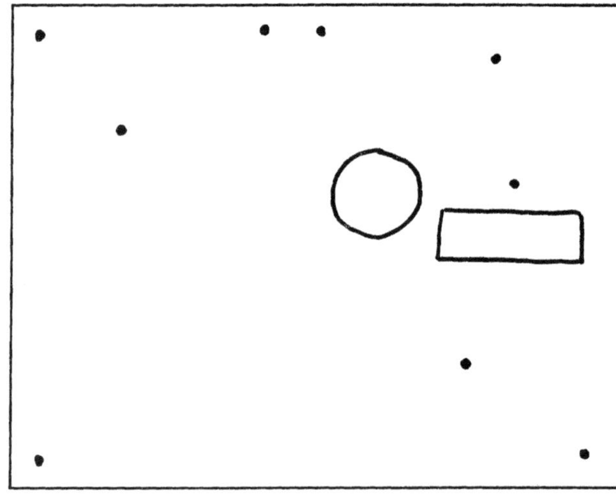

The set-up drawing

Somewhere to the left of the rectangle, but fairly close to it, I'll want you to draw a circle about the size of a Ping-Pong ball. Draw the circle now.

Now, it's time to make some dots.

Your first dot should go near the top left corner of your paper. It shouldn't touch the corner, it should just be close to it. Make the dot now.

Next, you'll be putting a dot a little bit down from the top edge of your paper, right in the center. Do this now.

And you'll be making another dot that is two finger widths to the left of the dot you just made. Draw that dot now.

Now there are dots to make in the bottom section of your paper.

First, you'll be making a dot near the bottom left corner but not touching it. Make the dot now.

Next, put a dot in the lower right corner of your paper, but not too close to it—maybe a couple of finger widths away from each edge. Draw it now.

Then, I want you to put a dot just a little above the rectangle you made. Do this now.

Finally, put three more dots anywhere you wish, but don't put them inside the circle or the rectangle.

SURPRISE! You've just started an interesting design!

We're going to begin by connecting some of the dots you just made. Using ten straight lines, connect some or all of the dots in any way you like. None of those lines can touch the rectangle or the circle, but they can cross each other.

Are you pleased with your design so far?

Now, it's time to bring the circle and rectangle into the design. Start by putting a dot in the middle of the circle. Then draw three straight lines to connect that dot to other dots.

Now, let's do something to the rectangle. Make three lines inside the rectangle. They can be short or curvy. They can cross each other. Just do something to make the three lines look nice inside the rectangle.

Here is the final direction. Connect each corner of the rectangle with any dot using curved lines. Your lines can cross other lines but they shouldn't touch the circle.

How does your masterpiece look? Try turning it around and viewing it from different sides. When you find the angle you like best, put your initials in the bottom right corner.

A finished version

Mystery Animal II

Say to students:

Position your paper so that one of the long sides is nearest to you, and don't do anything unti you've heard my instructions.

First, bring the bottom edge of your paper to the top edge and make a fold. Then smooth the paper back out.

Next, you'll be making a tiny dot. You should put it on the fold line, a little more than four finger widths in from the left edge of your paper. Make the dot now.

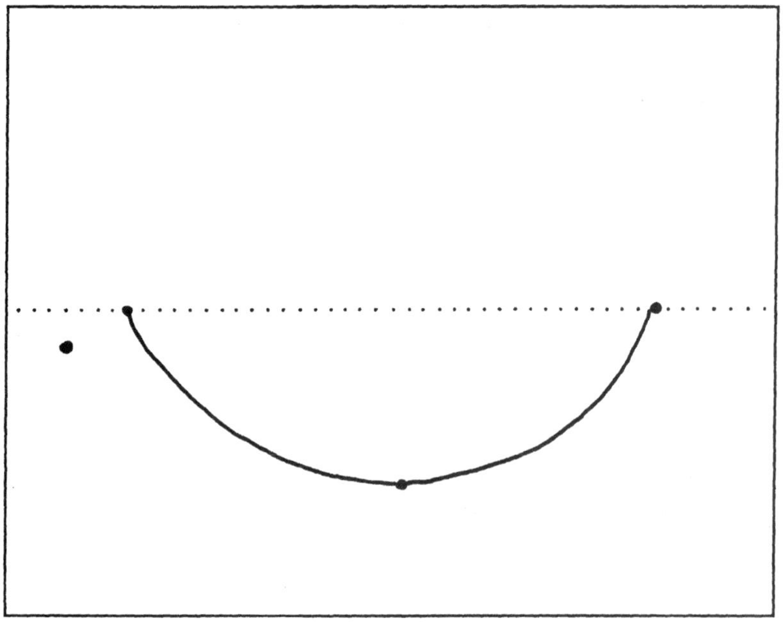

Now, you'll be making another tiny dot on the right side of your paper. It should also be on the fold line. Put it a little more than four finger widths in from the right edge. Make the dot now.

Next, I'll want you to make still another small dot. You should put it half way between the fold line and the bottom edge of your paper, about in the middle. Make the dot now.

The set-up drawing

Now, you'll be drawing a big smile. It should start at the left dot, touch the lower dot and end up at the right dot. Draw the smile now.

Finally, I'll want you to make one more dot. But this one should be a bit larger than the other dots. Where you put it is important, so listen carefully. It should be two finger widths in from the left edge of the paper and two finger widths down from the fold line. Make the dot now.

SURPRISE! Turn your paper upside down and you'll find that you've just started drawing a turtle.

The curved shape is the turtle's shell and the dot is the turtle's eye. Give the turtle a head, and then draw a line to form the bottom of the turtle's shell.

This turtle is walking, so you'll need to show its four legs. By the way, turtles' legs are short and thick and their feet are flat on the bottom. Draw the legs and feet now.

Turtles have tails that are quite short. Give yours a tail now.

Now, what else can you do to this turtle? Well, it has to be walking on something. Is it on pavement, or in the grass? How about working more on its eye? And will your turtle have a mouth? How about giving its shell more details? Turtle shells have interesting patterns. Good luck!

A finished version

Lou's Twos

Say to students:

Position your paper so that one of the long sides is nearest to you, and listen carefully to my directions before you do anything.

First, bring the bottom edge of your paper up to the top edge and make a fold. Then, smooth the paper out.

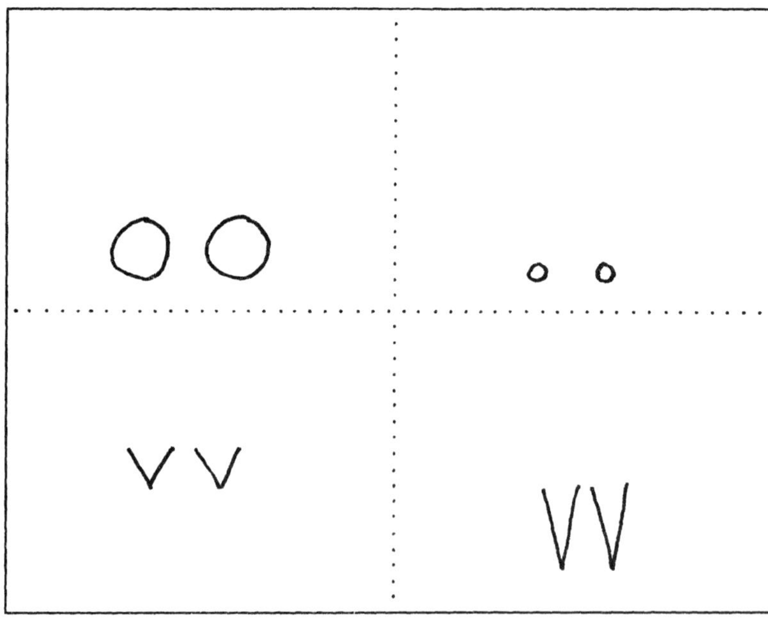

The set-up drawing

Then, fold the paper in half once more, left to right, and smooth it back out.

Be sure that one of the long sides is still nearest to you. Your paper is now divided into four rectangles, isn't it?

In the upper left rectangle, you'll be drawing two circles next to each other. They should each be about the size of a dime, and there should be about a thumb's width of space between them. You should put them near the bottom of the rectangle, in the middle. Draw the two circles now.

In the upper right rectangle, you'll be putting two more circles in about the same position as you put the other ones, with a thumb's width of space between them. But these circles should be half the size of a pea. Remember, they should be near the bottom of the rectangle, in the middle. Draw the two circles now.

In the lower left rectangle, in the middle, you'll be making two letter V's. They should be about as tall as your thumbnail. There should be a little bit of space between them. Draw the two V's now.

In the lower right rectangle, you'll be making two V's again but these should be tall and skinny. In fact, they should be about twice as tall as the first ones. There should be a little bit of space between them. Put them in the middle again but lower down than the other V's you just drew. Draw the two tall, skinny V's now.

SURPRISE! You've just started drawing a page from a photo album belonging to a boy named Lou.

Lou is going to tell you what's in each picture. It'll be your job to use the marks you just made as part of your picture. But there is one rule: Your drawings should not touch the fold lines or the edges of the paper.

Here is his description of the upper left photograph. "At the parade, I saw a clown with a big floppy hat riding a bicycle."

This is what he has to say about the upper right photograph. "My friend Jim is tall and skinny and he loves to ride his skateboard."

Here is his description of the lower left photograph. "My sister and I are eating snow cones."

And this is his description of the lower right photograph. "At the zoo, I saw a walrus with long tusks and a bunch of whiskers."

Now, draw around each of the pictures to make them look more like photographs in an album. And, if you want to add more details to your pictures, that's fine!

A finished version

Driving in the Desert

Say to students:

Place your paper so that one of the short sides is nearest to you, and listen to each instruction before you do any drawing.

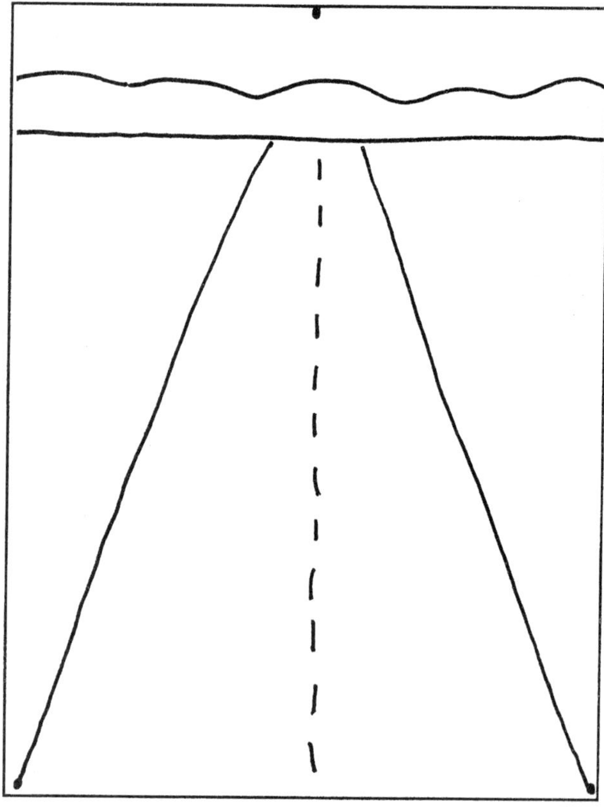

The set-up drawing

To begin this activity, you'll be putting a small dot at the top edge of your paper, right in the middle. Do this now.

Now, four finger widths down from the top edge of your paper, you'll be drawing a straight line that goes all the way across your paper, from the left edge to the right edge. Draw the line now.

Next, find the middle of that straight-across line you just made and put the point of your pencil there. Then, listen carefully. From the place where your pencil is, you will be making a line of little dashes that goes straight down to the bottom edge of your paper. Remember, the line should consist of short little dashes. Make the line now.

Next, you'll be putting a tiny dot in the bottom left corner of your paper. Do this now.

From the dot you just made, your next job will be to draw a line that goes toward the center dot at the top of your paper. The line should stop, though, when you reach the straight-across line in the top part of your paper. Draw the line now.

Now, you'll be putting another tiny dot in the bottom right corner of your paper. Do this now.

Then, from the dot you just made, you are to draw a line that goes toward the dot at the top of your paper but stops at the straight-across line. Draw the line now.

Now, half way between the top edge of the paper and the straight-across line, you'll be making a wavy line that goes all the way across the paper, from the left edge to the right edge. The line should go up and down like gentle waves on the ocean. Draw the line now.

SURPRISE! You've just started a drawing of a lonely highway in a desert with mountains in the distance.

First, let's concentrate on those mountains—that area above the straight-across line. How could you make the mountains look more real? Well, some mountains are always in front of other mountains. Can you think of a way to show that?

Of course, the big shape in the middle of your paper is the highway and the line with dashes is the center of the highway. As the highway gets closer to the mountains, it looks narrower, doesn't it?

There are only two cars on the highway. One is so far away it looks very tiny. The other car is closer to the bottom and looks bigger. Draw them.

Now think about this: What does a desert really look like? What's in a desert? Sand, sagebrush, armadillos, cacti and lots of other things. Add some desert details now. Good luck!

A finished version

The Very Old Tree

Say to students:

Position your paper so that one of the short sides is nearest to you, and listen carefully to each instruction before you do anything.

We're going to begin this activity today by doing something quite different. You'll be putting the hand you don't write with in the middle of your paper with your fingers spread out. Your fingers should point toward the top of the paper. Do this now.

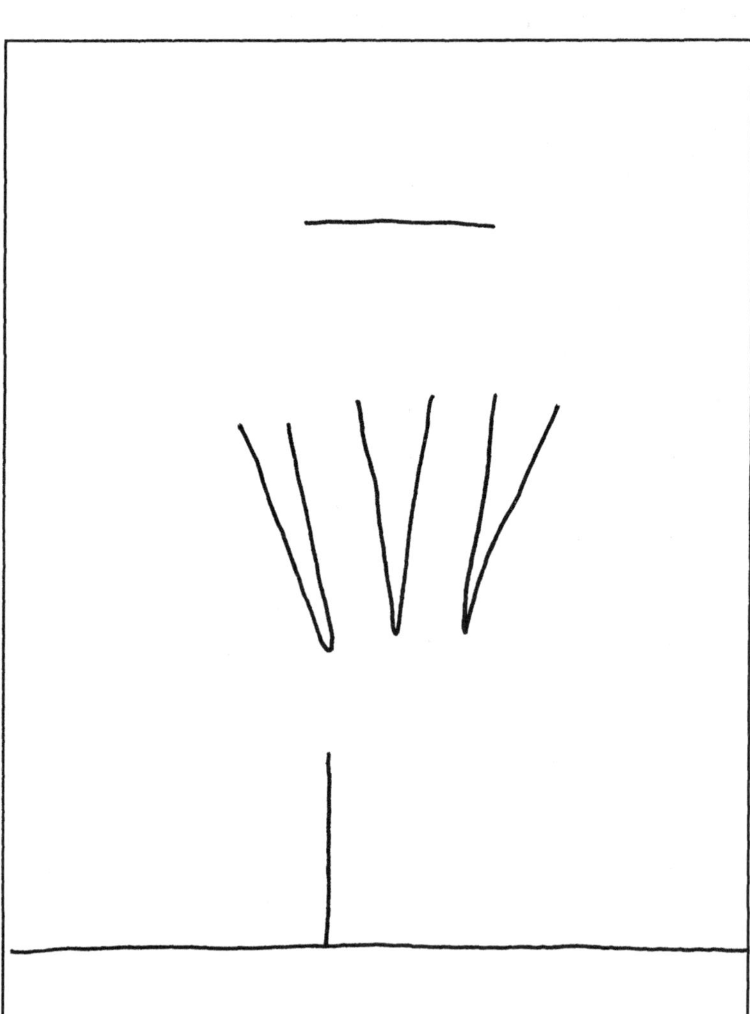

The set-up drawing

Next, you'll be drawing along the inside part of your fingers—not the top of your fingers and not your thumb. When you finish, you should have three skinny V shapes formed by the shapes between your fingers. Make the V shapes now.

Now, go to the bottom part of your paper, where you'll be drawing a line all the way across. Your line should start at the left edge of the paper, about two finger widths up from the bottom. Draw the line now.

See the V shape on the left? Your next job will be to draw a line that starts two finger widths below the bottom of the left V and goes straight down until it meets the straight-across line. Do this now.

Now, go back to the top of your paper. You'll be drawing a straight-across line about four finger widths wide. It should go about half way between the V's and the top of the paper. Draw this line now.

SURPRISE! You've just started a drawing of a very old tree.

The long up-and-down line on the left is one side of its thick trunk. Draw the other side.

The V's are the spaces between the main branches, but before you work on the branches, let me tell you what that line is above the V's.

That line is the floor of a tree house some kids have made. Draw the outline of the tree house now. You can finish it later.

Next, go ahead and draw the branches of the tree. Make sure some of the branches look like they are holding up the tree house. And make the branches go all the way out to the edges of your paper because this tree is so big you can't see all of it.

Okay, now you're on your own to put in some more details.

First, finish the tree house. Then, how about adding a ladder to get up to the tree house? Or maybe you'd like to draw a swing that hangs from one of the branches. And think about birds and flowers and grass. It's all up to you.

A finished version

A Rainy Day

Say to students:

Turn your paper so that one of the long sides is nearest to you, and don't do any drawing until you listen to my instructions.

First, a little more than half way up your paper, you'll be making a line that goes all the way across the paper, from the left edge to the right edge. Draw the line now.

Now, you'll be drawing a rectangle. It should be on the line somewhere in the left part of your paper. The rectangle should be about three finger widths wide and two finger widths tall. You won't need to draw the bottom side of the rectangle, since it will be formed by part of the line you have already drawn. Draw the rectangle now.

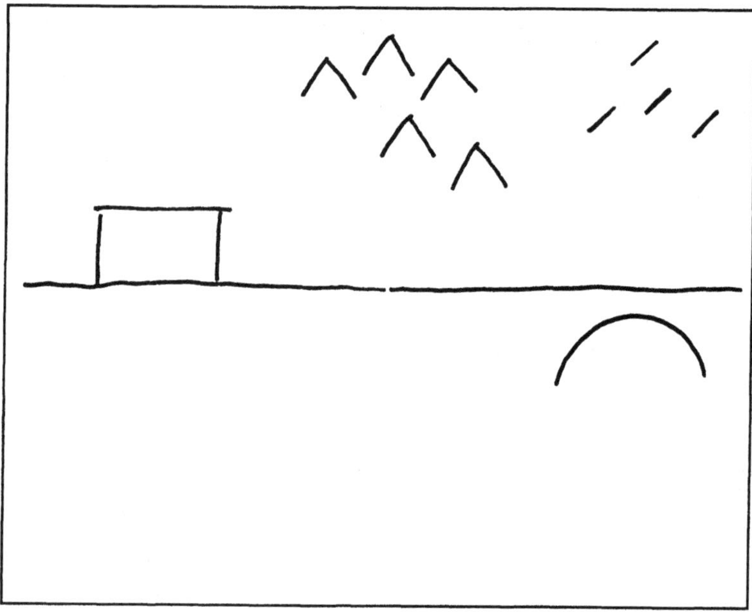

The set-up drawing

Next, in the upper right corner of your paper, I'll want you to make four short lines that slant in the direction of the bottom left corner. Each of the lines should have a little space around them. Draw the four short lines now, and remember to slant them in the direction of the bottom left corner.

Next, toward the top of your paper, near the center, I'll want you to scatter five little upside-down V's. They should be about as tall as your fingernail. They don't have to be in a row, but they should be near the top of the paper, in the center. Make the five upside-down V's now.

Now, on the right side of your paper, a little below the straight-across line, you'll be making an upside-down smile about the size of the rectangle you made. Do this now.

SURPRISE! You've just started a picture of a rainy day.

The rectangle on the left is a house. Give it a roof, some windows, and a door.

The upside-down smile is really the top part of an umbrella. Finish it and put somebody under it who is trying to stay dry.

The upside-down V's in the sky are the tops of pine trees on a hill behind the house. Finish the pine trees and make a hill for them to stand on. The hill line can go all the way across the paper if you wish.

Oh, I did say it was raining, didn't I? Those lines in the upper right corner are raindrops, of course. Add some more raindrops and also show a path that leads from the person up to the door of the house. Then add any other details you'd like to finish the scene.

A finished version

The Teddy Bear

Say to students:

First, position your paper so that one of the short sides is nearest to you.

In the middle of the paper, make a little X.

Next, bring the bottom edge of the paper up to the X and make a fold. Then, unfold the paper and smooth it out.

Now, bring the top edge of the paper down to the X and make a fold. Then, smooth the paper out. You have made three sections, haven't you?

Now, listen carefully to my instructions before you draw. In the middle of the top section, you'll be making a big oval that is a bit wider than it is tall. The top of the oval should almost touch the top of your paper. The bottom of the oval should come down to the top fold line. Remember, it should be wider than it is tall. Make the oval now.

Next, you'll be making another oval that looks just like the first one except that this one will be much smaller. It should be about as big as a raisin and it should go right in the middle of the bigger oval. Draw the small oval shape now.

Now, shade in the small oval to make it look dark.

We're still not quite finished with the small oval. The next thing you'll be doing is to make an upside down V that touches the bottom of the small oval, in the middle. It should be about as tall as the small oval. Make the upside-down V now.

Next, look at the bottom fold line. About three finger widths in from the left edge of the paper, on the fold line, you'll be making a little dot. Make the dot now.

Now, you'll be making another dot directly below the first dot. It should be about three finger widths below the first dot. Make the second dot now.

Then, starting at the top dot and ending up at the bottom dot, I want you to make a big letter C. Do this now.

Finally, in the middle section, you'll be making an oval shape that is so big that its top touches the top fold line and its bottom touches the bottom fold line. The oval should be taller than it is wide. Make the oval now.

SURPRISE! You've just started a drawing of a teddy bear!

The bear already has a nose and a mouth, but he'll need eyes and little round ears. Finish his face now.

The big oval, of course, is the bear's body, and that C you drew is one of his feet. Finish the bear's bottom legs now so it looks like he is sitting down with his legs spread. Then draw his other legs too. On teddy bears, two of the legs look more like arms, don't they? Go ahead and draw them now.

Here's the final challenge: The child who owns this teddy bear often dresses him up for fun. The teddy bear is wearing a particularly attractive outfit today—short pants with straps and big buttons, and a little bow tie around his neck. Show the teddy bear wearing these clothes now, and add whatever other details you want. Good luck.

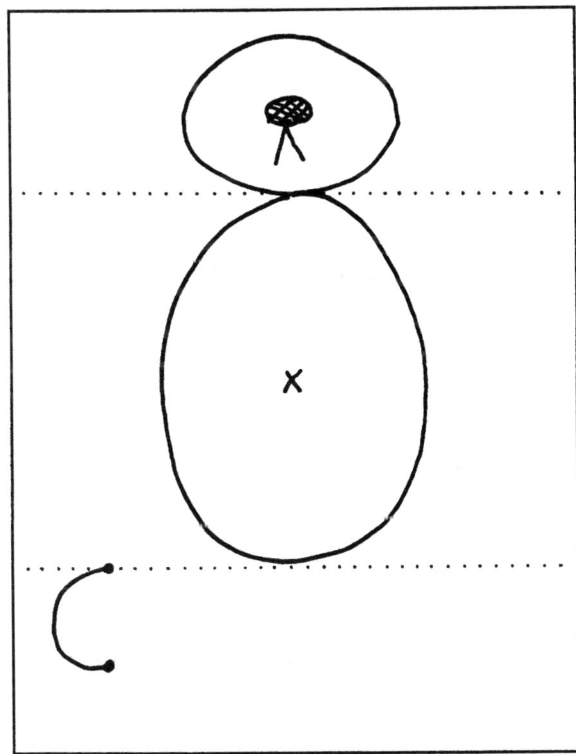

The set-up drawing

A finished version

Bubbles

Say to students:

Position your paper so that one of the long sides is nearest to you, and don't draw until you hear my instructions.

First, about three finger widths from the bottom of your paper, I'll want you to draw a straight line across your paper, from the left edge to the right edge. Draw the line now.

Next, you'll be making a tiny dot. You should put it on the line you just drew, about four finger widths in from the right edge of your paper. Make the dot now.

Now, measure straight up from that dot about as high as your pointer finger. Place your pencil there. That is where I'll want you to make a circle about the size of a pea. Make the circle now.

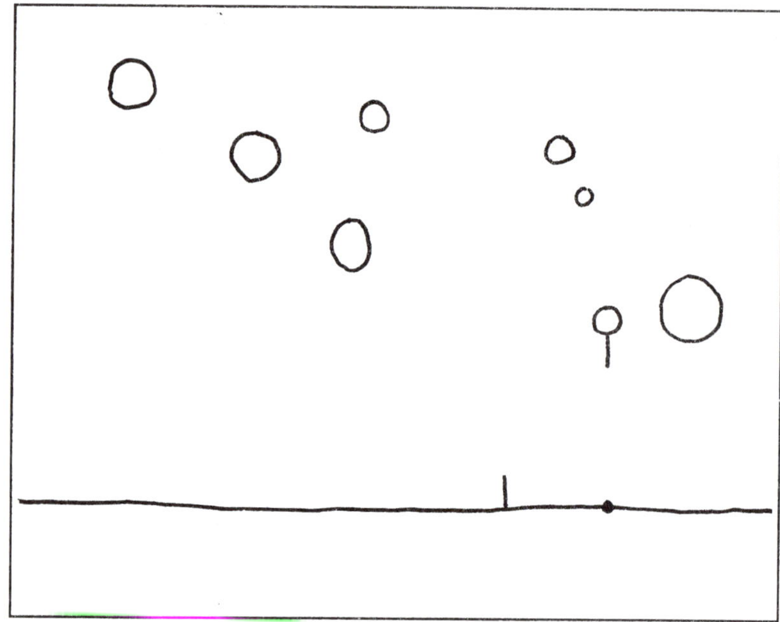

The set-up drawing

Next, you'll be drawing a short line about as long as your little fingernail. It should come out of the bottom of the circle, in the middle, and go straight down. Make the short line now.

Now, about one finger width to the right of the circle, you'll be drawing a bigger circle. It should be about the size of a penny. Draw the bigger circle now.

Next, go back to the dot. About two finger widths to the left of the dot, still on the line, you'll be drawing an up-and-down line about as tall as your little fingernail. Remember, it should start at the line and go up. Draw it now.

Finally, in the top half of your paper, draw six circles of different sizes. None of them should be bigger than a grape, but don't make any of them exactly the same size. Scatter them out.

SURPRISE! You've just started a drawing of a child blowing bubbles!

The up-and-down line with the circle on it is the bubble ring, the little plastic piece that you dip into the soap bottle.

The bigger circle is the head of the person blowing bubbles. Show that person holding the bubble ring now.

The little line coming up from the straight-across line is one side of the jar that holds the bubble solution. Finish drawing the jar.

Now, draw some bubbles coming out from the bubble ring and rising toward the circles you drew. Of course, the circles are also bubbles.

There is some grass growing up from the line, which is the ground. A big bubble has landed in the grass but it has not yet popped. Show the grass and the bubble.

Then, think of some other things you can add to your picture. Are there some double bubbles or even some triple bubbles floating in the air? Is there a dog watching the bubbles being blown? Are there birds in the sky? You decide. Good luck.

A finished version

Schoolwork

Say to students:

Place your paper so that one of the short sides is nearest to you, and listen to my instructions before you do anything.

First, bring the bottom edge of your paper up to the top edge and make a fold. Then, smooth the paper out.

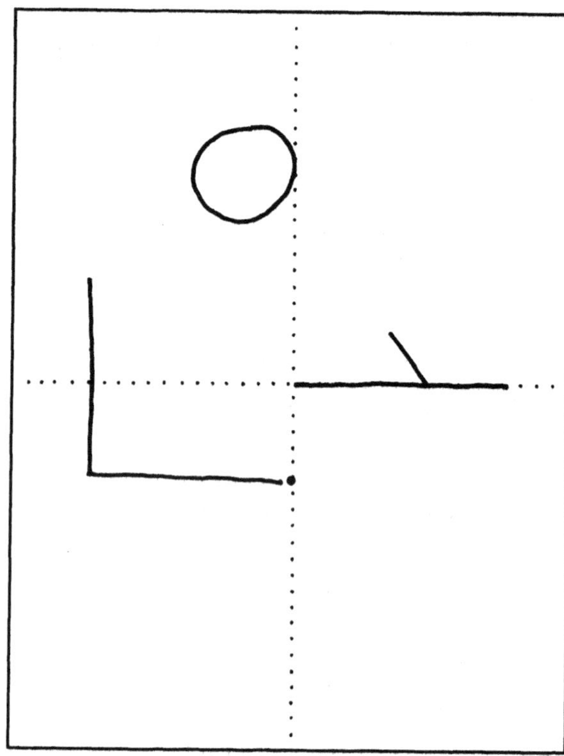

The set-up drawing

Next, bring the left edge of your paper to the right edge and make a fold. Then, smooth the paper out.

Now, starting at the place where the fold lines meet, you'll be drawing a straight line that goes toward the right edge of the paper, along the fold line. The line should stop about three finger widths from the edge. Draw the line now.

Next, go back to the center. You'll be measuring down three finger widths and making a tiny dot. The dot should be on the fold line. Do that now.

Your next job will be to make a straight line that goes from the dot toward the left edge of the paper. It should stop three finger widths from the edge. Make the line now.

Starting at the left edge of the line you just made, you'll be making a line that goes straight up. The line should be about as long as the straight-across line that you're starting from. Remember, it should go straight up. Do that now.

Then, you'll be making a circle about the size of a Ping-Pong ball. Its right side should touch the up-and-down fold line, half way between the center of your paper and the top edge. Draw the circle now.

Next, go back to the line that starts at the very center of your paper. Put your pencil point on that line about half way across. You'll be drawing a short line that goes in the direction of the circle. It should only be as long as the width of your thumb—in other words, not very long. Draw that short, slanted line now.

SURPRISE! You've just started a drawing of a person sitting at a desk doing schoolwork!

Now let me tell you what all those lines on your paper mean.

The big L shape is the back and seat of the chair the person is sitting on, the circle is the person's head, the straight line across is the desktop, and the short slanted line is a pencil the person is writing with. Your job will be to use all of these things in your drawing of a student doing schoolwork.

And when you finish doing all of that, which isn't easy, think of other things you could put in your picture—a clock on the wall, windows—you decide. Good luck.

A finished version

Parachute Jump

Say to students:

Position your paper so that one of the long sides is nearest to you, and don't do anything until you listen to my instructions.

On the right side of your paper, about three finger widths in from the edge, you'll be drawing a line that starts at the top of your paper and goes all the way down to the bottom. Draw the line now.

Next, go to the top left corner of your paper. Measure three finger widths over from the left edge and three finger widths down from the top edge and make a dot. Now, starting at the dot, you'll be making a line that goes straight down. It should be about two finger widths long. Draw the short line now.

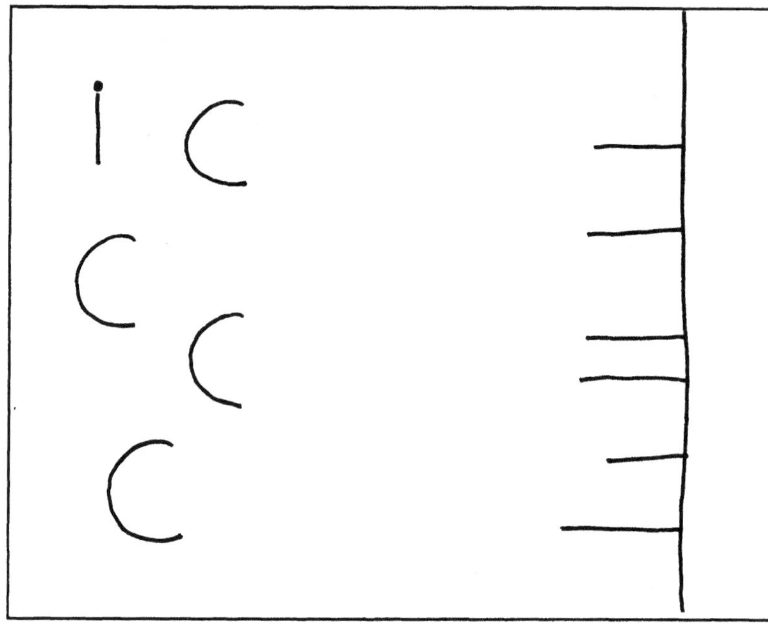

The set-up drawing

Next, on the left side of your paper, but not touching the short line you just drew, I'll want you to make four large C's. The C's should be about as tall as the short line. Scatter them around in that area, but don't put them side by side. Remember, they should be put on the left side of your paper. Make the four C's now.

Next, go back to the long line, and listen carefully. You'll be making six straight lines, two or three finger widths long, that start at the up-and-down line and point toward the left side of the paper. Space them out along the line any way you wish. Draw the six straight lines now.

SURPRISE! You've just started a drawing of a skydiving adventure!

The first thing to do is to tip your paper so that a short side is now nearest to you. Which short side? The one with the line drawn all the way across.

Now, let's finish the picture.

That little short line you see in the top right corner is part of an airplane that the skydivers have jumped from. Finish drawing the airplane now.

The line down at the bottom is the ground, and the lines coming up from the ground are tree trunks. Turn them into complete trees.

Now for the important part—the skydivers. The C's, which are now upside-down U's, are really open parachutes. Your job is to finish drawing the parachutes and show little people hanging from them.

Look! One skydiver has just jumped from the plane and he hasn't opened his parachute yet. His arms and legs are spread out. Be sure to show a little parachute strapped to his back.

A finished version

Finally, think of other things you could do to make this picture action-packed. Has one of the parachutists just landed? Is another one on the ground and walking around? Is one of them about to land on a tree? The more details the better—you decide!

Roasting Marshmallows

Say to students:

Position your paper so that one of the long sides is nearest to you, and listen to my instructions before you draw.

The first thing I'll want you to do is to put a tiny dot on the left edge of your paper. You should put it about half way between the top and bottom of the paper, right on the edge. Make the dot now.

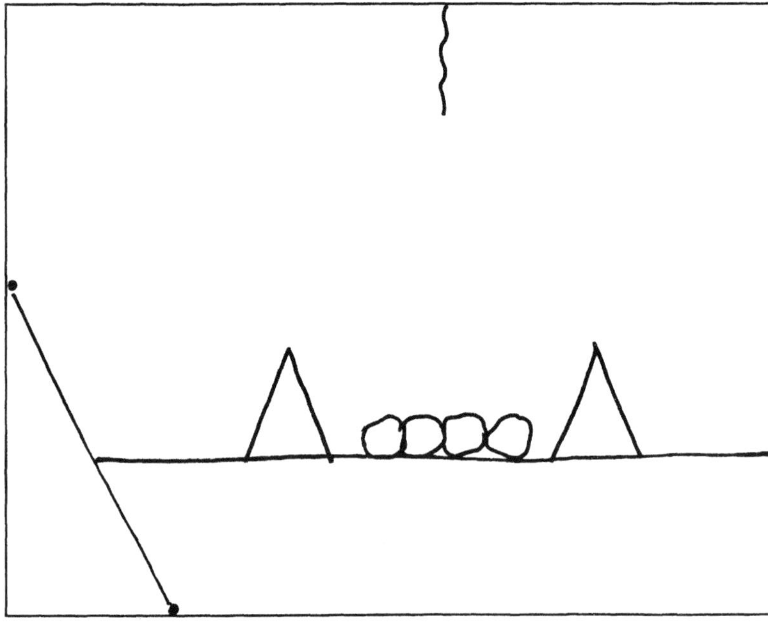

The set-up drawing

Now, you'll be making another tiny dot. This one should go on the bottom edge of your paper, a little more than four finger widths over from the left edge. Make the dot now.

Next, draw a straight line connecting the dots.

Now, place the point of your pencil about in the middle of the line you just made. From there, I'll want you to draw a line straight across to the right side of your paper. Draw the straight-across line now.

Next, on top of the straight-across line, about in the middle, you'll be drawing four lumpy-looking circles, about the size of dimes. They should be put in a row, and they should touch each other. Draw the lumpy circles now.

Now, starting near the middle of the top edge of your paper, you'll be drawing a short wiggly line that comes straight down toward the lumpy circles. It should be about three finger widths long. Draw the wiggly line now.

Next, go back to the line where the lumpy circles are. I'll want you to put one upside-down V slightly to the left of the circles and one upside-down V slightly to the right of the circles. The V's should be as tall as your little finger, and they should be on top of the straight-across line. Make the two upside-down V's now.

SURPRISE! You've just started a drawing of two stick people roasting marshmallows.

The four little lumpy circles are some of the rocks that have been put around the fire, but the fire itself is missing. Draw some firewood and a small fire.

By the way, that little line at the top is part of the smoke coming up from the fire. Make the line come all the way down to the fire, and add three or four more lines if you desire.

I said these were stick people, didn't I? What are stick people? They have circles for heads but the rest of their bodies are made out of lines, and those upside-down V's are their legs. They're standing close to the fire because they're roasting marshmallows on sticks right now. In other words, the stick people are holding sticks, and on the end of the sticks are marsh-mallows. Show how that would look.

That slanted line at the left is part of a big tent. You can't see it all, because most of it is out of the picture. It needs a door—at least part of a door—to make it look more like a tent. Draw part of the door and put a stick person inside looking out.

Uh-oh. That stick person on the left has kept his marshmallow over the fire too long. His marshmallow is now black and a little bit of smoke is rising from it. Show how it looks.

A finished version

Finally, what else can you do to make the drawing more interesting? How about adding more stick people? How about a stick dog? How about some stick trees? Put in as many details as you can. Good luck!

The Everything Drawer

Say to students:

Position your paper so that one of the long sides is nearest to you, and don't do any drawing until you hear my instructions.

Your first job will be to draw a large rectangle that fits just inside the shape of your paper. The lines you make should be about a finger width away from the edge of your paper. Draw the large rectangle now.

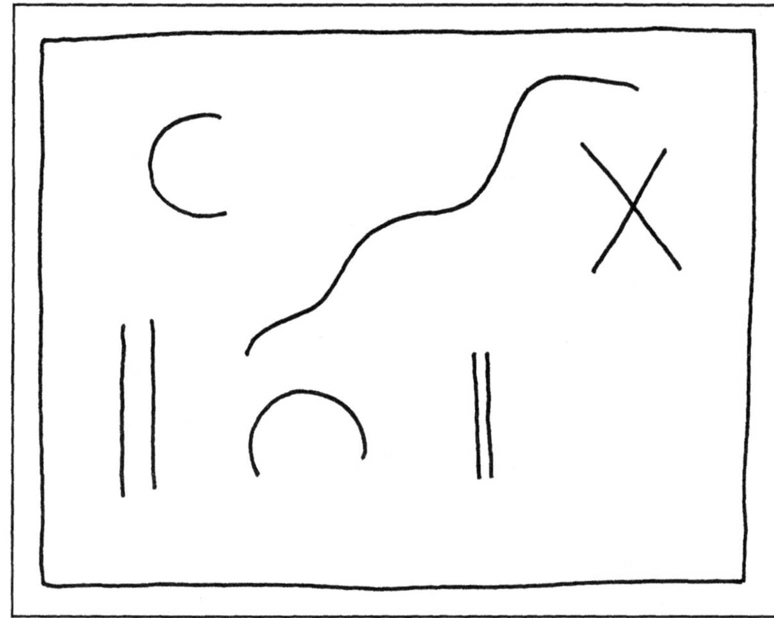
The set-up drawing

Next, listen carefully. The rest of the instructions involve drawing things inside the big rectangle. You can draw them anywhere you wish inside the rectangle, but each thing you draw should not touch any other thing. In fact, be sure that there is some space around everything you draw. Ready?

To begin, I'll want you to make an X that is about as high as your little finger. Do this now.

Next, you'll be making a letter C that is about three finger widths tall. Do this now.

Then, you'll be making another letter C about the same size as the first one. This one is tipped on its side, with the open end facing down. Draw it now.

Next, you'll be drawing two up-and-down lines about as tall as the X. They should be very close together but not touching. Draw them now.

Now, I'll want you to draw two more close-together up-and-down lines. These lines should be a little taller than the other ones you just drew. The lines should also be a little wider apart, about a finger width of space between them. Draw them now.

Your last job will be to draw a line with several curves in it. The line should be about as long as one of the short sides of your paper. Remember, it shouldn't touch anything else.

SURPRISE! You've just drawn the beginning of an everything drawer!

Do you have an everything drawer in your house? You know, it's that drawer that collects all sorts of odd things—things you have tossed there when you're in a hurry and don't have time to put in a better place.

Here is what all the funny lines are:

The shorter pair of straight up-and-down lines is the beginning of a pencil. The pencil has a very sharp point. There is an eraser at the other end, too. Finish it.

The first C you drew is part of a roll of tape. Draw the roll of tape now.

The other C is the top part of a light bulb. Finish it. (If you put the C too close to something else, go ahead and draw another one in a different place and use it to make the light bulb. You can turn the other C into some other thing later.)

The X is really the beginning of a pair of scissors. Turn the X into a pair of scissors.

The taller up-and-down lines are the sides of a flashlight. Finish it.

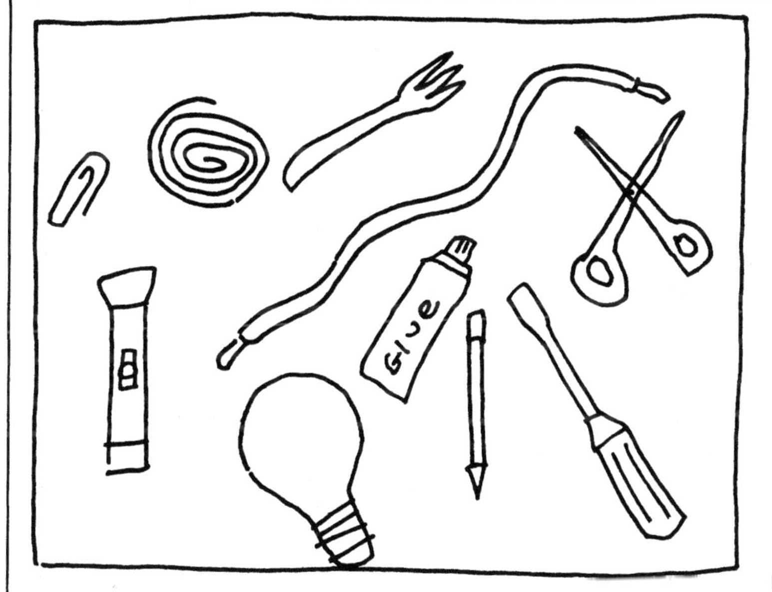

A finished version

The long wiggly line is one side of a shoelace. Make the shoelace look fatter by drawing another line beside the first line, and remember that a shoelace always has tips at its ends.

Finally, can you think of other things that might show up in an everything drawer? How about paper clips, screwdrivers, nails, safety pins? You decide, then go ahead and make sure you fill up that drawer!

Index

Publications by Tin Man Press

Is It Friday Already? — 30 weeks of learning centers in nine subject areas.

Are They Thinking? — A comprehensive, year-long thinking-skills program.

Loosen Up! — Art activities designed to build confidence.

T is for Think — More than 300 drawings spur thinking excitement.

OPQ — Offbeat Adventures With the Alphabet — Center approach based on the alphabet.

Waiting for Lunch — Quick activities for those little moments in the day.

Great Unbored Bulletin Board Books I and II — 20 great board ideas in each book.

Great Unbored Blackboard Book — Quick analytical activities you do on the board.

WakerUppers — 50 friendly hand-drawn reproducible sheets motivate thinking.

Nifty Fifty — 500 provocative questions about 50 everyday things.

Smart Snips — Each of the 50 reproducible activities starts with something to cut.

Ideas To Go — 50 assignments cover a broad range of thinking skills.

Brain Stations — 50 easy-to-make centers encourage creative thinking.

Play by the Rules — 50 scripted challenges turn students into better listeners.

Going Places — Students participate in five interesting listening adventures.

Letter Getters — Letter clues promote language development and deductive reasoning.

Letter Getters II — One hundred more challenging word puzzles.

Just Write! — 50 activities get children writing in spite of themselves.

Gotta Think! — An entertaining assortment of 50 thought-provoking activity sheets.

Surprise in the Middle — Innovative listening activities have a visual outcome.

How Would That Look? — Students follow precise drawing instructions.

The Discover Series — 24 card sets provide hands-on experiences with everyday objects.

The Think About Series —12 card sets use familiar subjects to spur creative thinking.

Adventures of a Dot Series — 10 card sets use a Dot character to encourage thinking.

Linework — Jumbo card set centers around the concept of line.

An Alphabet You've Never Met — Jumbo card set plays creatively with letters.

Phone: (800) 676-0459 **Fax:** (888) 515-1764

www.tinmanpress.com